CALENDAR HISTORY

A MATH LESSON

www.math2kids.com

An interesting book that will teach children and those not so young to know all the steps that have been taken to have the calendar that we currently use. Calendar that helps us to carry out in an organized way all the activities of our daily life

We cannot imagine how we could carry out our daily activities without being able to measure time. We would not know when and at what time we should carry out our activities.

8:30 Reading
9:45 Math
AY 2010
W TH F S
4 5 6 7
11 12 13 14
18 19 20 21

To measure periods of time less than a day, man invented the clock.

And in order to measure periods greater than one day, man invented the calendar.

DO	LU	MA	MI	JU	VI	SA
1	2	3	4	5	6	7
8	9	10	11	12	13	14
15	16	17	18	19	20	21
22	23	24	25	26	27	28
29	30	31				

Before the calendar existed, farmers did not know on what dates they should start sowing. For this reason, their crops seldom bore fruit, as sometimes their crops were lost due to snow, and other times they dried up due to lack of rain.

People did not know how old he was because they did not know what day they were born, therefore they did not know when his birthday would be.

How old are you ?
I don’t know, I think that zero

Nor could they celebrate any important date or event, because they did not know what date things happened. That's why Santa Claus never came.

The solar day

The first way to tell time was day and night. The time that has elapsed since the sun rises, sets, and rises again is known as a solar day. The solar day is the basis for measuring time and is the reference used in the calendar. Time is measured based on how many days have passed or how many times the sun has risen since a certain event occurred.

The lunar calendar

The ancient peoples of Mesopotamia were the first to measure longer periods of time. These peoples began to use a 30-day calendar based on the phases of the Moon.

And when is your baby going to be born?
in 2 full moons

The Mesopotamians discovered that it always takes 15 days for the Moon to go from a Full Moon (which is when the Moon is bigger) to a New Moon (which is when the Moon is not seen) and that takes another 15 days for the Moon to go from New Moon to Full Moon again.

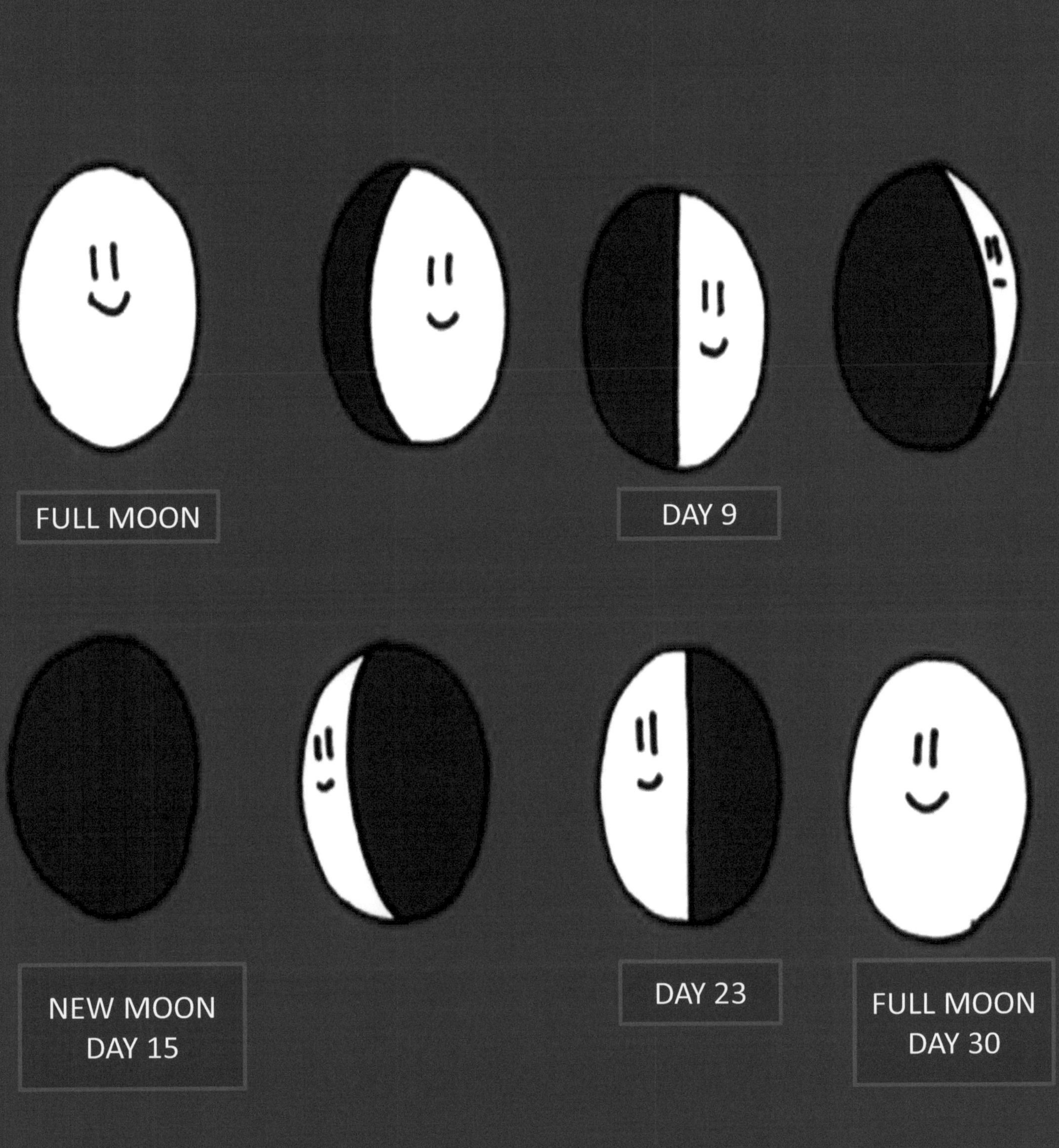
FULL MOON
DAY 9
NEW MOON
DAY 15
DAY 23
FULL MOON
DAY 30

Egyptian solar calendar

The Egyptians to know when they had to cultivate their lands invented the solar calendar 3,000 years before our current era. This calendar is based on the time it takes for our planet to make one complete revolution around the Sun.

The Egyptians discovered that the Spring Equinox occurred every 365 days, which is when day and night have the same length. And that from that date the plants began to bloom. This system is the same that we continue to use to count the years!

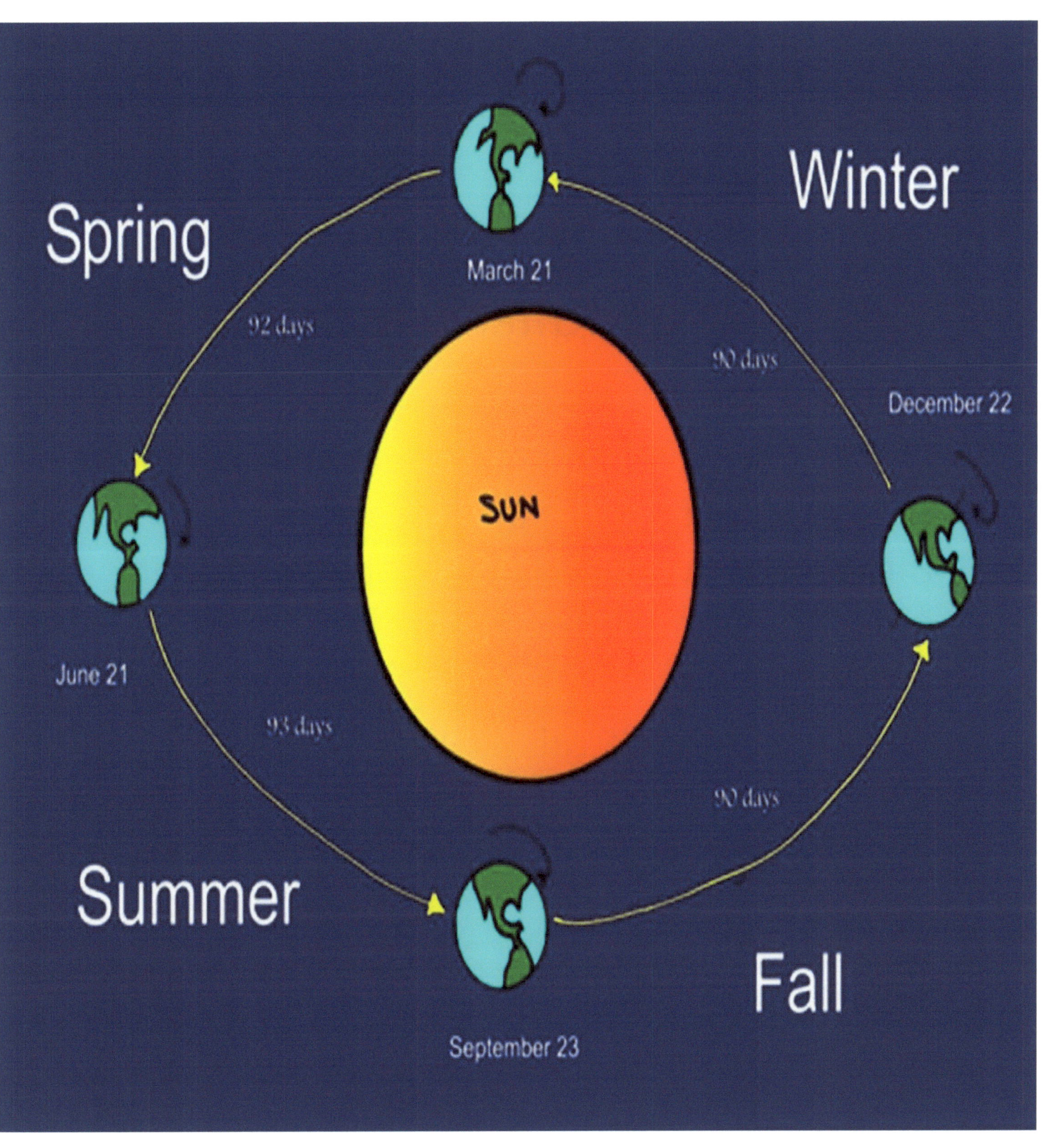
Spring
March 21
Winter
92 days
90 days
December 22
SUN
June 21
93 days
90 days
Summer
Fall
September 23

Roman or Julian calendar

The Romans during their conquests copied the Egyptian calendar and spread it throughout Europe. In 46 BC, the Romans in order to control shorter periods of time divided the 365-day Egyptian solar calendar into 12 lunar calendars which they called months. The Roman calendar began in the month of March.

Name of the Roman months

Mes	Roman name	dedicated to :	English name
1	Martius	Marte God	March
2	Aprilis	Month in which the flower open	April
3	Maius	Month of abundance	May
4	Iunius	Juno God	June
5	Iulius	Julio Cesar emperor	July
6	Augustus	Augusto emperor	August
7	Septembris	Month seven	September
8	Octobris	Month eight	October
9	Novembris	Month nine	November
10	Decembris	Month ten	December
11	Iannarius	Jano God	January
12	Februaris	Februa or purification	February

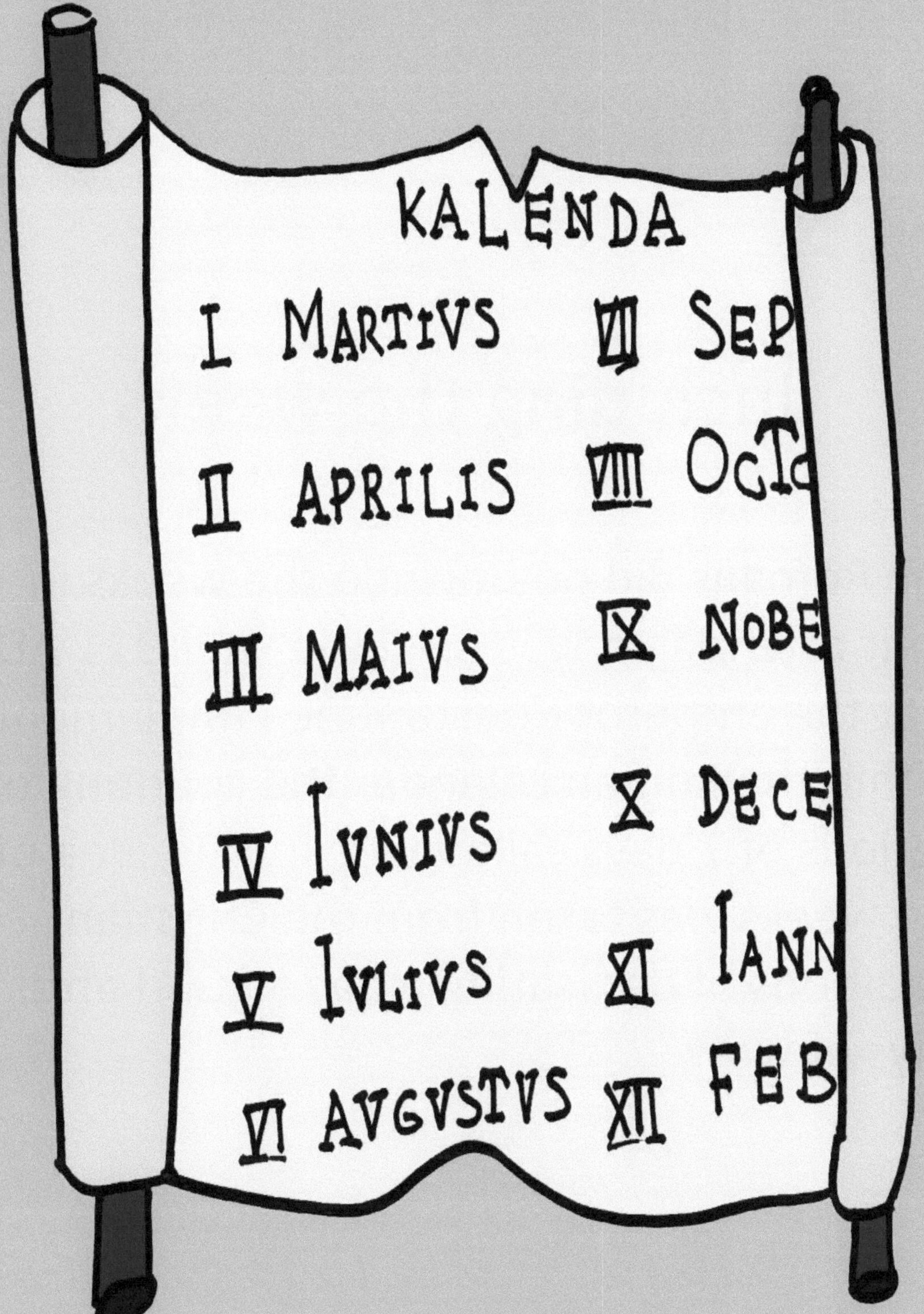

KALENDA

I MARTIVS

II APRILIS

III MAIVS

IV IVNIVS

V IVLIVS

VI AVGVSTVS

VII SEP

VIII OCTO

IX NOBE

X DECE

XI IANN

XII FEB

Including the weeks

The Romans did not include the weeks in their calendar, it was until the year 321 AD that the emperor Constantine I implemented within the Roman calendar the counting of periods of 7 days called weeks. The idea of the weeks was taken from the Christian traditions of dedicating a day to God after 6 days of work.

The names of the days of the week were taken from the Latin names of some Astros.

Roman name	dedicated to	English name
Diu solis	the Sun	Sunday
Luna	the Moon	Monday
Martis	planet Mars	Tuesday
Mercurii	planet Mercury	Wednesday
Jovis	planet Jupiter	Thursday
Veneris	planet Venus	Friday
Saturni	planet Saturn	Saturday

LVNIVS CCCXXI

SOLIS	LVNA	MARTIS	MERCVRII	JOVIS	VENERIS	SATVRNI
I	II	III	IV	V	VI	VII
VIII	IX	X	XI	XII	XIII	XIV
XV	XVI	XVII	XVIII	XIX	XX	XXI
XXII	XXIII	XXIV	XXV	XXVI	XXVII	XXVIII
XXIX	XXX					

Gregorian or current calendar

The calendar we use today was designed in 1582 AD by a group of mathematicians from the University of Salamanca Spain. And it was prepared at the request of Pope Gregory XIII who wanted the Roman calendar used at that time to coincide with the Christian religious holidays, that is why they chose the beginning of the calendar in the month of January since it was the closest full month to the birth of Christ.

The current calendar begins in the month of January.

They changed the starting month of the calendar but did not change the order and names of the months so as not to further confuse users at that time. This caused that the names of the following months to no longer agreed with the meaning of its name:

Actual Name	Meaning of Roman Name	order in actual calendar
September	month 7	month 9
October	month 8	month 10
November	month 9	month 11
December	month 10	month 12

January

SUN	MON	TUE	WED	THU	FRI	SAT
				1	2	3
4	5	6	7	8	9	10
11	12	13	14	15	16	17
18	19	20	21	22	23	24
25	26	27	28	29	30	31

February

SUN	MON	TUE	WED	THU	FRI	SAT
1	2	3	4	5	6	7
8	9	10	11	12	13	14
15	16	17	18	19	20	21
22	23	24	25	26	27	28

March

SUN	MON	TUE	WED	THU	FRI	SAT
1	2	3	4	5	6	7
8	9	10	11	12	13	14
15	16	17	18	19	20	21
22	23	24	25	26	27	28
29	30	31				

April

SUN	MON	TUE	WED	THU	FRI	SAT
			1	2	3	4
5	6	7	8	9	10	11
12	13	14	15	16	17	18
19	20	21	22	23	24	25
26	27	28	29	30		

May

SUN	MON	TUE	WED	THU	FRI	SAT
					1	2
3	4	5	6	7	8	9
10	11	12	13	14	15	16
17	18	19	20	21	22	23
24	25	26	27	28	29	30
31						

June

SUN	MON	TUE	WED	THU	FRI	SAT
	1	2	3	4	5	6
7	8	9	10	11	12	13
14	15	16	17	18	19	20
21	22	23	24	25	26	27
28	29	30				

July

SUN	MON	TUE	WED	THU	FRI	SAT
			1	2	3	4
5	6	7	8	9	10	11
12	13	14	15	16	17	18
19	20	21	22	23	24	25
26	27	28	29	30	31	

August

SUN	MON	TUE	WED	THU	FRI	SAT
						1
2	3	4	5	6	7	8
9	10	11	12	13	14	15
16	17	18	19	20	21	22
23	24	25	26	27	28	29
30	31					

September

SUN	MON	TUE	WED	THU	FRI	SAT
		1	2	3	4	5
6	7	8	9	10	11	12
13	14	15	16	17	18	19
20	21	22	23	24	25	26
27	28	29	30			

October

SUN	MON	TUE	WED	THU	FRI	SAT
				1	2	3
4	5	6	7	8	9	10
11	12	13	14	15	16	17
18	19	20	21	22	23	24
25	26	27	28	29	30	31

November

SUN	MON	TUE	WED	THU	FRI	SAT
1	2	3	4	5	6	7
8	9	10	11	12	13	14
15	16	17	18	19	20	21
22	23	24	25	26	27	28
29	30					

December

SUN	MON	TUE	WED	THU	FRI	SAT
		1	2	3	4	5
6	7	8	9	10	11	12
13	14	15	16	17	18	19
20	21	22	23	24	25	26
27	28	29	30	31		

Today the measurement of time in seconds, minutes, hours, days, weeks, months, and years are indispensable tools in our daily lives. Thanks to the calendar we know how old we are and when our birthday is.

Farmers know what dates to sow to get the best harvests.

Thanks to the calendar we know what days we go to school and when we go on vacation ...

And also, among many other things, thanks to the calendar we never forget the dates of our favorite holidays.

END

Other Math Stories from Math 2 kids

1.- The number One
2.- Full moon
3.- The 3 friends
4.- The 3 friends jump in bed
5.- The colors of the farm
6.- The 3 friends and the fierce eraser
7.- The 3 friends go fishing
8.- The troop
9.- The 5 explorers
10.- Let's go to the amusement park
11.- The first day of school
12.- And where is the hamster?
13.- The numbers go in order
14.- The order is important
15.- How is my name spelled?
16.- The day of taking the photo.
17.- Bar graph
18.- The number One birthday
19.- Color patterns
20.- Our friend the number Zero
21.- The world of figures
22.- The circle is important
23.- Let's invite the figures to play
24.- A parade of figures
25.- A world of colors
26.- Drawing with figures
27.- Zeronderella
28.- The one that is a ten
29.-A trip to the country of tens
30.- The 100th day of school
31.- Sorting food
32.- 1, 5, 10 and 25 cents
33.- The numbers play the clock
34.- More and Less
35.- The Equal sign
36.- Learning to add
37.- Adding is better
38.- Greater and less than
39.- Odds against pairs
40.- Measurements
41.- Playing to measure
42.- My credit card
43 The units go to a field day

- 44.- To change the old bus
- 45.- Playing with the domain
- 46.- Our store
- 47.- Teensnow white and the 7 dwarfs
- 48.- When they were taller
- 49.- Pedro's 3 wishes
- 50.- A tale of how the numbers were invented
- 51.- The value according to its position
- 52.- The power of number 10
- 53.- Magic Table
- 54.- Roman numerals
- 55.- Two Little Red Riding Hood
- 56.- A race to count
- 57.- The history of the calendar
- 58.- The seasons of the year
- 59.- How to use the calendar
- 60.- The history of the clock
- 61.- The Five learn to multiply
- 62.- Learning to use the clock
- 63.- Story of how the money was invented
- 64.- A very hard working penny
- 65.- An unexpected gift
- 66.- Learn to divide in a way fun in a week
- 67.- Multiplying with manipulatives
- 68.- Story to multiply
- 69.- And what is the perimeter?
- 70.- It was a story measuring that terrain
- 71.- How to calculate any area
- 72.- A cake for Milly
- 73.- The Venn diagram
- 74.- The coordinates of a story
- 75.- The Story of how the fractions were invented.
- 76.- Halves, fourths and eighths
- 77.- Adding fractions
- 78.- A trip to the country of tenths
- 79.- The day we won the lottery
- 80.- It is a game of probabilities

In Amazon

MATH 2 kids

A math lesson about fractions, based on a beautiful story that tells us what the teacher Mily did to evenly distribute among her assistants the numbers One, Two, Four, and Eight the cookies, juice, cakes, and pizzas that were leftover from the winter party. Additional to the tale it also includes a complete Math lesson on fractions.

DIVIDING FRACTIONS
A MATH LESSON

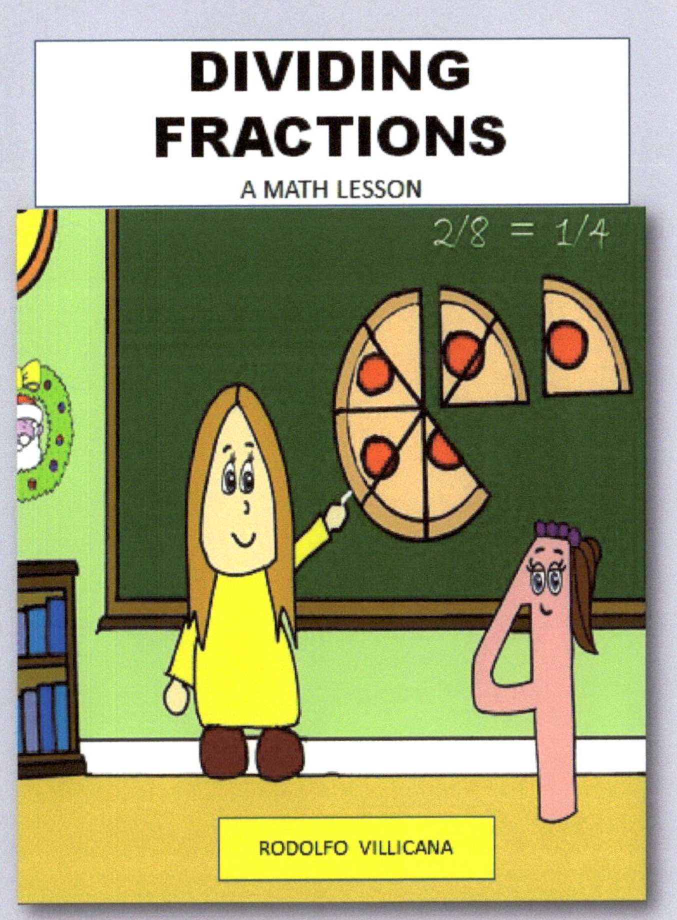

www.ingramcontent.com/pod-product-compliance
Ingram Content Group UK Ltd.
Pitfield, Milton Keynes, MK11 3LW, UK
UKHW060121300726
14090UKWH00002B/304

* 9 7 9 8 5 2 7 1 9 0 3 9 7 *